FRANCIS POULENC

SONATA : 1922

for Flute and Guitar

Transcribed from the Sonata for Horn
Trumpet and Trombone
by
Gregg Nestor

CHESTER MUSIC

à Mademoiselle Raymonde Linossier

SONATA
(1922)

FRANCIS POULENC
arranged for Flute and Guitar by
Gregg Nestor

Flute part edited by
Gordon Halligan

1. Allegro moderato

2. Andante

FRANCIS POULENC

SONATA : 1922

for Flute and Guitar

Transcribed from the Sonata for Horn
Trumpet and Trombone
by
Gregg Nestor

CHESTER MUSIC

à Mademoiselle Raymonde Linossier

SONATA
(1922)

FRANCIS POULENC
arranged for Flute and Guitar by
Gregg Nestor

Flute part edited by
Gordon Halligan

1. Allegro moderato

Flute

2. Andante

3. Rondeau

Francis Poulenc (1899-1963) composed in a style that could be called distinctly French. He was the true *'bon vivant',* and his works display elegance, wit and sophistication combined with an inherent gift of melody.

The **Sonata (1922),** originally for Horn, Trumpet and Trombone is dedicated to Mademoiselle Raymonde Linossier, a childhood friend of the composer with exceptional intelligence and culture who initiated him into the world of literature.

In adapting this early work for flute and guitar, I felt that the peculiar traits and jollity of this music together with its occasional biting dissonances would translate especially well in this format.

Gregg Nestor,
Los Angeles, May 1985

Also available:
Poulenc: **Mouvements Perpétuels**, transcribed for Flute and Guitar by Arthur Levering (CH55441)

10

3. Rondeau

Francis Poulenc (1899-1963) composed in a style that could be called distinctly French. He was the true *'bon vivant'*, and his works display elegance, wit and sophistication combined with an inherent gift of melody.

The **Sonata (1922),** originally for Horn, Trumpet and Trombone is dedicated to Mademoiselle Raymonde Linossier, a childhood friend of the composer with exceptional intelligence and culture who initiated him into the world of literature.

In adapting this early work for flute and guitar, I felt that the peculiar traits and jollity of this music together with its occasional biting dissonances would translate especially well in this format.

Gregg Nestor,
Los Angeles, May 1985

Also available:
Poulenc: **Mouvements Perpétuels**, transcribed for Flute and Guitar by Arthur Levering (CH55441)

GUITAR SOLOS

Guitar Solos from France, Italy, Jacobean England and Spain (ed. Gilbert Biberian), 4 vols.

Lennox Berkeley	— **Guitar Concerto**, reduction for guitar and piano (ed. Julian Bream)
Lennox Berkeley	— **Sonatina** (ed. Julian Bream)
Lennox Berkeley	— **Theme and Variations** (ed. Angelo Gilardino)
Gilbert Biberian	— **Columbine:** a choreographic suite
Manuel de Falla	— Two Dances from **The Three-Cornered Hat** (arr. Siegfried Behrend)
Manuel de Falla	— **Homenaje:** Le Tombeau de Claude Debussy (revised edition by John Duarte)
Manuel de Falla	— Two Pieces from **El Amor Brujo** (arr. Emilio Pujol)
Thea Musgrave	— **Soliloquy I** for guitar and tape
Joaquin Rodrigo	— **Sonata Giocosa**
Alec Rowley	— **Miniature Preludes and Fugues** (arr. José de Azpiazu)
Igor Stravinsky	— Allegro from **Les Cinq Doigts** (arr. Theodore Norman)

GUITAR DUETS

Guitar Duets from the Renaissance (ed. Gilbert Biberian)
Guitar Duets, Music of Four Centuries (arr. Mary Criswick)

Gilbert Biberian	— **Pierrot:** Suite No. 1
Manuel de Falla	— Two Dances from **The Three-Cornered Hat** (arr. Graciano Tarrago)
Francis Poulenc	— **Mouvements Perpétuels** (arr. Arthur Levering)
Igor Stravinsky	— Eight Pieces from **Les Cinq Doigts** (arr. Theodore Norman)

GUITAR TRIOS

Guitar Trios, Music of Four Centuries (arr. Mary Criswick)

GUITAR QUARTETS

Guitar Quartets (ed. Gilbert Biberian), 2 vols.

CHESTER MUSIC

Exclusive distributors:
Hal Leonard
7777 West Bluemound Road, Milwaukee, WI 53213

Email: info@halleonard.com
Hal Leonard Europe Limited
42 Wigmore Street Maryleborne, London, WIU 2 RY
Email: info@halleonardeurope.com

Hal Leonard Australia Pty. Ltd.
4 Lentara Court Cheltenham, Victoria, 9132 Australia
Email: info@halleonard.com.au